T0149005

The English Castles Story

The English Castles Story

Marc Alexander

The History Press

Published in the United Kingdom in 2016 by
The History Press
The Mill · Brimscombe Port · Stroud · Gloucestershire · GL5 2QG

Copyright © The History Press, 2016

The right of Marc Alexander to be identified as the Author of
this work has been asserted in accordance with the Copyright,
Designs and Patents Act 1988.

All rights reserved. No part of this publication may be
reproduced, stored in a retrieval system, or transmitted, in any
form, or by any means, electronic, mechanical, photocopying,
recording or otherwise, without the prior permission of the
publisher and copyright holder.

British Library Cataloguing in Publication Data
A catalogue record for this book is available from the British
Library.

Hardback ISBN 978-0-7524-9110-3

Typesetting and origination by The History Press
Printed in China

Half title: Sudeley Castle.
Half title verso: Thornby Castle.
Title page: Scarborough beach with the castle in the distance.
(FreeImages.com/Lewy Ryan)
Front cover: Leeds Castle. (FreeImages.com/Eva Halsdorfer)
Back cover: Corfe Castle. (FreeImages.com/martinclay)

HISTORY IN STONES

In *As You Like It* Shakespeare wrote of 'sermons in stones'. 'History in stones' would be an apt phrase to describe the castles that have not only reflected the most turbulent episodes in Britain's history but played significant roles in it. Yet it was not until after the Norman Conquest that castles, as we think of them, came into being.

Before them there were Iron Age hill forts surrounded by deep trenches and timber palisades, providing protection for local tribes. Some of these earthworks have survived and had the name 'castle' grafted on to them. An example of this is the prehistoric hill fort known as Cadbury Castle, which stands impressively on the Somerset plain. It is a contender for the site of King Arthur's legendary Camelot.

Britain's first stone-built strongholds are the mysterious brochs which, according to archaeological estimation, were built in Scotland as early as 100 BC. A broch was a circular tower with several floors and walls that curved inward and enabled the 'dry-stone' structure to rise to heights of over 40ft. Such was the skill of the broch builders that their works have been described as 'some of the most sophisticated examples of dry-stone architecture ever created'. It is thought that they were the fortified dwellings of local chieftains and places of safety from raiders.

Today there remain over 500 sites with ruins of these amazing forerunners of castles.

A further step towards castles came after England became part of the Roman Empire in AD 43 and the Romans proved their expertise in building with dressed stone from local quarries. This was demonstrated after the Emperor Hadrian visited Britain in AD 120 and work began on the great wall that bears his name. One of the most distant frontiers of the Empire, it stretched 70 miles between Wallsend in the east and Barrow-on-Solway in the west and is regarded as one of Rome's most remarkable building achievements.

Small watchtower-style forts were built at intervals along the wall and today some of their ruins remain and are known as milecastles.

While the Romans did not build castles as such, they did construct forts in strategic places such as river crossings or in defensive locations. For example, commanding forts were sited along the eastern and southern English coast as defence against

Saxon invaders. Of these strongholds guarding what became known as the Saxon Shore, Burgh Castle is regarded as one of Britain's most impressive Roman relics.

After the Romans abandoned Britain early in the fifth century, the Saxons did invade. Despite the efforts of heroes personified by the legendary King Arthur, England became divided into Anglo-Saxon kingdoms, often at war with each other. And then the Normans came with their genius for castle building.

Today the castles that were built across the country after the Conquest, whether well preserved or reduced to romantic ruins, remain milestones in English history. It is estimated that there are over 400 of these and each would be worth a book in itself. However, in this book the castles mentioned have been selected to portray various aspects of the English castles story.

The great age of castle building in England was heralded by Edward the Confessor's enthusiasm for everything Norman. He was born the son of King Æthelred and Emma of Normandy in 1003. Thirteen years later the English crown passed to Canute and Edward became a royal exile in Normandy, where he developed a warm friendship with William, the son of Robert III, Duke of Normandy.

In 1042, the English throne became vacant and Edward was invited to return and accept the crown, which he did with the support of Earl Godwine, the foremost noble in the kingdom. In due course Edward married the earl's daughter, Edith.

The new king's admiration of the Normans soon became evident. Norman clerics were invited to settle in England and Norman French became the language of the court, where Norman favourites were deeply resented by the English nobility.

Meanwhile Edward's excessive piety – experiencing holy visions and curing ailments with his touch – earned him the title of the Confessor.

His saintliness was to have a far-reaching effect as his marriage to Edith was never consummated. Before coming to the throne he had made a holy vow of lifelong chastity, with the result that there would never be a royal heir to the crown.

When William, now Duke of Normandy, visited the English court, the childless Edward promised his old companion that he would be his royal successor.

In 1064, Harold Godwinson, the king's brother-in-law was in a vessel that violent winds blew on to the French shore at Ponthieu. The following events – so vital in English history – are depicted in the brilliant embroidery of the Bayeux Tapestry.

Count Guy de Ponthieu, a vassal of Duke William, seized Harold, no doubt in the hope of ransom money. When Duke William learned that the son of the foremost English noble in England was a prisoner he ordered him to be brought to Rouen. The two men got on well, Harold even accompanying William on a military expedition in Brittany, and he was honoured for his gallant support. William then asked Harold to swear to support his claim to the English throne and to 'be his man' when the time came.

Harold agreed to make the vow at a table on which was a leather box known as a phylactery. When the ceremony was completed he was shown that the box contained holy relics and therefore he had sworn a holy oath. He was then allowed to return to England.

Towards the end of 1065 King Edward lay dangerously ill. Anxious over the succession, he broke his promise to Duke William and is said to have whispered that Harold Godwinson, the scion of England's most powerful family, should be the next king. The Witan supported this and after Edward died a few days later Harold became the anointed King of England, his excuse over his vow to William being that it had been made under duress – he was technically William's prisoner – and it was therefore invalid.

When news reached William that Harold had been crowned he began his preparations to invade England.

His problem was that England was a more powerful state than the Duchy of

Normandy and with its large Anglo-Saxon population he would not have enough Norman troops for the campaign. He therefore informed Pope Alexander II that the new king of England had broken a vow sworn on holy relics, a crime against God and the Church. He added that if he succeeded in winning what was rightfully his he would build a cathedral in gratitude (a promise he was to keep).

In reply the Pope endorsed his claim and sent him a papal banner, which in fact meant that the invasion would be a righteous crusade. When news of this spread, knights from different countries rallied to William's banner, eager for the benefits that would come with victory. By the time William's army was ready he had 2,000 knights from Normandy and other European states at his command.

On 27 September, William's Viking-style boats set out from St Valery. As well as war horses, they carried prefabricated forts – a portent of what lay ahead. They consisted of wooden sections shaped so that they could be fitted together quickly. The Bayeux Tapestry shows one that was taken to Hastings, being hastily assembled on a mound. Three years later it was granted to Robert, Count of Eu, who replaced the wooden defences with masonry, and thus the first Norman castle was built in Britain.

Although William had lived up to his sobriquet of the 'Conqueror', he did not yet have control of England. Although on Christmas Day 1066 he was enthroned in Westminster Abbey, the masterwork of The Confessor, the ceremony did not endear him to his new subjects. Revolts broke out, the best remembered led by

AN ENGLISH CASTLE WAS
BOMBARDED BY GERMANS

Like so many castles, Scarborough had its place in English history – such as when it was held by Edward II's favourite, Piers Gaveston. When the king's enemies captured the castle, Piers was taken to Warwick Castle where it was decided to behead him due to the influence he had upon king. Scarborough Castle was to suffer various sieges but its most dramatic hour came in 1914, when it first experienced modern warfare. On 16 December, two German warships, the *Derfflinger* and the *Von der Tann*, fired an estimated 500 shells at Scarborough town and the castle, which was severely damaged. Today it is a Scheduled Ancient Monument in the care of English Heritage and has become a popular tourist attraction.

Hereward the Wake, the word 'Wake' meaning 'the watchful one'.

William's answer to insurgency was the castle. The castle provided a fortified base for the local commander's troops to sally forth in response to unrest before it spread. Therefore the country was divided into vast estates – known as fiefs – dominated by castles under the control of barons, the warriors and knights who were thus rewarded for their services in the 'crusade'.

Each baron held his fief as a tenant of the king in return for the service of his knights when required. In turn these knights were tenants of the baron. Their tenants were the serfs who were granted a few acres of land. Thus every man was in the service of someone above him, with the king at the apex of the pyramid. The system became known as the feudal system, from the word 'fee', meaning estate.

Because of the enmity of the Anglo-Saxon English, it was vital that castles should be erected across the country as quickly as possible. Strategic sites were chosen in commanding positions on high ground or hilltops.

Where there was no natural suitable site a great circular ditch would be dug with the spoil piled in the centre to create an artificial mound. On top of this a stronghold would be built with a wall bordering the defensive ditch, everything being constructed of wood. The central mound was known as the motte and the area within the encircling stockades was the bailey.

As time passed many of these wooden motte and bailey 'castles' were reconstructed in stone and some have lasted to this day.

When King William died in 1087, over eighty Norman-style castles had been built.

LINCOLN CASTLE

So determined was William the Conqueror to build a strategic castle at Lincoln that over 150 domestic dwellings had to be demolished to provide a site for the construction. The first dramatic incident in the castle's history occurred in 1141 when King Stephen attempted to capture it, but it was he who was captured outside the castle walls. He was held a prisoner of his cousin Queen Matilda until he was exchanged for her half-brother, enabling him to resume the throne.

In 1217, Lady Nicola de la Haye was constable of the castle when there was a

rebellion by a number of barons angered by King John disregarding the terms of the recently signed Magna Carta. Seeking military help, the barons aligned themselves with Prince Louis of France. His army occupied the city of Lincoln and besieged the castle. Thanks to the gallant leadership of Lady Nicola, the defence was so successful that after forty days the siege was abandoned. This was said to have saved England from French rule.

Later the castle was used as a prison, which was closed in 1878. Now, in the twenty-first century, it has been given a new lease of life with restoration work costing millions of pounds.

◄ Lincoln Castle standing proud after significant restoration work. (iStock.com/Batukman)

Apart from the new motte and bailey castles which were being erected across England, King William – according to the chronicler William of Poitiers – 'realised it was of the first importance to overawe the Londoners'. The answer was the construction of the Tower of London, which was not only a mighty fortress but a palace. With this symbol of royal authority overawing the city, William's next great project was Windsor Castle.

THE TOWER OF LONDON

For the location of what was to become the world's most famous castle, the newly enthroned William chose the south-east corner of London's Roman wall, overlooking the Thames. This was ideal for his purpose. In 912 his Norse ancestor, Rollo Ragndvalsson, had led Viking ships up the Seine to menace Paris. Charles III of France – known as the Simple – bought off the threat by giving the Northmen land stretching from the coast to within 30 miles of Paris. This became the Duchy of Normandy. William therefore wanted a fortress overlooking the river as a safeguard against a similar invasion.

The strategic value of the site had long been recognised. It is believed that Julius Caesar built a fort there – certainly there are Roman foundations beneath the Tower – and Alfred the Great later built a stronghold on the spot.

To oversee the project, William chose a remarkable monk named Gundulf who, having studied Saracen architecture when he was in Jerusalem, had gained a reputation as an inspired builder. Work began on what was to become known as the Jewel Tower, and as recognition of his effort Gundulf later became Bishop of Rochester and went on to build Rochester Cathedral.

For the sake of speed, timber was the original building material. Then, in 1078, William's Norman masons built a great three-storey keep with a concentric wall surrounding it. William II carried on the work after his father's death in 1087 and while the interior did not have the comfort of later royal residences, its banqueting hall and Council Chamber meant that it was not just another fortress.

More improvements came when, in 1189, Richard I went crusading and the kingdom was put in the care of William Longchamp, Bishop of Ely. With Prince John scheming to replace his brother, the bishop spent great sums of money on improving the Tower's defences as a bastion loyal to the absent king. Its area was doubled, deeper moat-type ditches were dug, sections of curtain wall were added and the Bell Tower was built.

These fortifications, however, did not deter John from besieging the castle. Although he was unable to take it by force, the bishop had to surrender due to lack of supplies.

In 1234, Henry III built the Great Hall and the Wakefield Tower. To improve the castle's appearance he had it whitewashed, thus giving it the name of the White Tower.

➤ Tower of London. (Freeimages.com/kamal babla)

Tower of London.
(FreeImages.com/Colin Cushman)

His castle-building son, Edward I, had a moat dug encircling the castle, whose water came straight from the Thames. He also built a new defensive wall so that if attackers managed to breach the outer wall they would find themselves facing another. These concentric fortifications ensured that the Tower was the most impregnable castle in the kingdom. Yet in 1381, during the Peasants' Revolt, a mob managed to enter the castle and behead Archbishop Sudbury and Sir Thomas Hales, the king's treasurer.

Over the years the castle was added to until it had the appearance we are familiar with today. Covering 18 acres it has thirteen towers apart from the White Tower within the inner wall. The last royal building work was carried out by Henry VIII. This was a row of timber-framed houses to act as lodgings when Anne Boleyn was crowned queen after her marriage to the king.

CAPTAIN BLOOD

Known in history as the man who nearly stole the Crown Jewels, the Irish adventurer Colonel Thomas Blood was on the Parliamentary side during the Civil War, with the result that he lost his estate at the Restoration. On the morning of 15 March 1671, dressed as a clergyman, he entered the Tower of London with three friends. On reaching the chamber where the royal regalia was kept, Blood felled the Keeper of the Jewels with a mallet he had secreted under his clerical robe. The quartet then made off with the crown and orb.

The alarm was raised, and the thieves were pursued and apprehended. While the penalty for such a crime would have been the gallows, Charles II, perhaps amused at Blood's audacity, visited the rogue in prison. He then granted him a pardon, a position at court, and returned his estate to him. Such royal benevolence led to the rumour that the king, who was always in need of money, had colluded with the reckless colonel in a plan to turn the regalia gems into hard cash for their mutual advantage.

▲ Tower of London. (FreeImages.com/Craig Makin)

charged him with treason and had him executed out of hand. Other prisoners with noble connections were executed on Tower Green, as it was considered improper that they should be executed like commoners on Tower Hill in front of a jeering mob. Today the spot on Tower Green where the scaffold was erected is marked by a plaque.

One of the most tragic figures to be led on to the Green was Queen Anne Boleyn, who was beheaded there on 19 May 1536. Tudor execution was performed by the headsman's axe but the manner of Anne's death was a novelty. Her considerate husband, Henry VIII, had a special executioner brought from Calais to decapitate her with a sword, a French custom unknown in England. Her body was interred in the Tower chapel of St Peter ad Vincula where other noble victims were buried.

Although the castle was both a palace and a fortress, its reputation as a prison was a chilling reminder that it had no respect for blood or position. In 1483, Lord Hastings was the first to die on Tower Green when Richard, Duke of Gloucester,

◄ Tower of London. (FreeImages.com/Philip Munro)

In 1542 Henry's fifth wife, Catherine Howard, was also beheaded in the Tower. When she was informed that the execution would take place the next day her response was to ask for the headsman's block to be brought to her cell to rehearse her part so she would be dignified in the grim ceremony.

In contrast Lady Salisbury was so terrified she tried to flee from the headsman and had to be forcibly made to kneel at the block. Another tragic victim was Lady Jane Grey, the nine-day queen.

While such executions were technically legal, there were several deaths and disappearances that became Tower folklore. Following the Battle of Tewkesbury in 1471, the deposed Henry VI was imprisoned in the Tower by the victor, Edward IV. On the night of 21 May that year he died, it was said, 'of pure displeasure and melancholy', though tradition suggests he was murdered while at prayer.

Seven years later George, Duke of Clarence, was accused of treason by his brother King Edward and imprisoned in the Tower, where he was said to have been drowned in a butt of Malmsey, his favourite wine.

The Tower's best known mystery is the fate of young Edward V and his brother

▲ Tower of London. (FreeImages.com/Philip Munro)

Richard, Duke of York, the sons of Edward IV – the so-called 'Princes in the Tower'. All that is known for sure is that after their father's death in 1483 they were placed in the Tower by their uncle Richard, Duke of Gloucester, and never heard of again. Although down the centuries Richard III has been regarded as his nephews' murderer, the truth of their disappearance still inspires argument.

The first celebrated victims of Henry VIII's break with the Roman Catholic Church were Sir Thomas More and John Fisher, Bishop of Rochester, who refused to accept the king as the head of the Church of England and were executed on Tower Hill in 1535. Four centuries later they were both canonised by the Pope.

The last person to be beheaded in the Tower was Simon Fraser, Lord Lovat, who, in 1747, paid the price for his part in the Jacobite Rebellion. The last prisoner in the Tower was the Nazi Rudolf Hess, who, in 1941, made a solo flight to Scotland, possibly to propose an Anglo-German peace pact.

Today, a governor resides in the sixteenth-century Queen's House on Tower Green. His work includes the supervision of the yeomen warders who, in their traditional Tudor uniforms, are popularly known as 'beefeaters'. They live within the Tower and their duties include conducting guided tours.

The Tower is designated a UNESCO World Heritage site and remains England's top tourist attraction, welcoming between 2 and 3 million visitors a year.

THE HEROINE OF CORFE

When the Civil War broke out, Corfe Castle was owned by the Royalist Sir John Bankes, the Attorney General. He was absent from the castle in 1643 when it was besieged by Parliamentarian troops. Lady Mary Bankes took control of the defence and held out valiantly for three dangerous years. The castle only fell due to the treachery of one of her officers, who opened the gates to the Roundheads. The victors then slighted the castle with barrels of gunpowder so that it was permanently ruined, but Lady Bankes and her children were given safe conduct to leave before her home was destroyed.

➤ Lady Mary Bankes.

WINDSOR CASTLE

Accurately described as 'an enduring symbol of Britain's royal heritage', Windsor Castle has been a royal castle ever since William the Conqueror had it built in the eleventh century. And after nine centuries it still is. Her Majesty Queen Elizabeth II spends private weekends there and it is traditionally her official residence during Royal Ascot week and Easter.

William had been King of England for four years when he decided to build it near the Thames, 25 miles west of London. The site the Conqueror chose was close to Old Windsor, once a Saxon settlement with a royal connotation. It was there that Edward the Confessor had a royal hunting lodge.

At first the castle was of the motte and bailey type, built as fast as possible in the newly conquered kingdom. When Henry II came to the throne in 1154 stone replaced wood when he built the Round Tower and constructed an encircling wall. Later, under the direction of Edward III, the castle was so improved that a contemporary chronicler wrote that 'there was not another more splendid within the bounds of Europe'.

According to the chronicler Holinshed, because Edward had been born in the castle and had great affection for it, he did not count the cost of adding beautiful buildings to it. It was here that he founded the Order of the Garter in 1348.

In turn Edward IV was responsible for the castle's magnificent chapel of St George, in which are the tombs of ten British sovereigns.

When Elizabeth I was resident in the castle, she had a long gallery constructed

➤ Windsor Castle. (FreeImages.com/ bugdog)

DURHAM CASTLE WAS ONCE A BISHOP'S PALACE

Durham Castle shares the honour of being a UNESCO World Heritage Site along with Durham Cathedral. It is appropriate as the castle, which was built soon after the Norman Conquest, became more than a stronghold when the king chose the Bishop of Durham to be his royal representative in the area, and thus Durham Castle became the bishop's palace. Many castles have become famous for their roles in rebellion, civil war and various military episodes. But not Durham. After the headquarters of the ruling bishops was relocated at Auckland Castle, Durham Castle became a famed centre of learning when it was turned into a prestigious college. Its scholastic reputation has continued from 1837, when the University of Durham was founded in its precincts.

➤ Durham Castle, long famed for being a seat of learning. (FreeImages.com/Emma Wolf)

➤ Windsor Castle.
(FreeImages.com/Aneta Pietura)

so that she could take walks whatever the weather. Later it was transformed into the castle library. It is said that Shakespeare wrote *The Merry Wives of Windsor* at her behest, and its first performance was held at the castle.

Although the castle was a royal residence rather than a fortress like the Tower of London, it did have its own 'historic' episodes.

It was from the castle that King John was forced by the barons to go to nearby Runnymeade to put his seal to the Magna Carta in June 1215. The king had no intention of respecting the conditions of the charter and he persuaded the Pope to excommunicate the barons. This ignited a civil war between the faction loyal to the Crown and the rebels opposed to John.

The latter petitioned Prince Louis, the Dauphin of France, to become their leader. After his arrival in England he besieged Windsor Castle but the attempt failed.

Later the castle was to hold royal captives – David Bruce, the King of Scotland, and John II, the King of France, after his capture at Poitiers. After the Battle of Edgehill the Parliamentarians took over the castle, which became the headquarters for Oliver Cromwell's army. Charles I was imprisoned there until his execution.

The castle had been neglected during the Civil War and John Evelyn wrote in his famous diary that it was 'exceedingly ragged and ruinous'. With the Restoration Charles II repaired the buildings, restored the royal apartments and employed Grinling Gibbons to provide wood carving. Outside an avenue was designed to enhance the Great Park, which was so enjoyed by Queen Anne that it became known as Queen Anne's Ride.

THE CASTLE THAT GOT BLOWN DOWN

Few castles can have had such a varied story as York Castle. After 1066 there was such resentment against the victors, exemplified by Hereward the Wake, that the Normans decided it was imperative to have a strong castle in North Yorkshire. Thus, in 1068 William the Conqueror built a motte-and-bailey castle at York. He chose a strategic location overlooking the River Ouse and the castle was speedily constructed of wood. William had faith in timber construction, having brought a prefabricated wooden castle to England when his army crossed the Channel.

When the work was completed in 1069, William had a second castle erected on the west bank of the river. In the same year a Viking raiding fleet sailed up the Humber and along the Ouse. This raid encouraged the local population to rise against their new masters and attack some castles. Norman retribution spread across Yorkshire and was underlined by rebuilding the castles.

As time passed, the second castle that William had built was demolished while improvements were made to the first. Later, in 1228, Yorkshire folk must have believed in divine retribution when it was blown down in a furious storm. Sixteen years later, Henry III, noted for his work on Westminster Abbey, decided to rebuild the shattered York Castle with stone rather than wood. For this ambitious project he employed the great castle architect Royal Master Mason Henry of Reynes to supervise the project, which took twenty-five years to complete.

This rebuilt castle is still famed for its design, which includes a keep that was known as the King's Tower. Later, the name was changed to Clifford's Tower, a name by which the castle is often known. The name is believed to go back to 1322, when the corpse of

Sir Robert Clifford and the bodies of other rebel Lancastrians were hung from its battlements. During a period of warfare between the English and the Scots, Edward I transferred his government to York Castle, making it the centre of national administration. Later, the castle took on a less dignified role, becoming a prison, where in 1739 the famous highwayman Dick Turpin was hanged.

Today York Castle, now a Scheduled Monument and with a world-famous museum, is in the care of English Heritage.

Clifford's Tower at York Castle. (FreeImages.com/Scheer Jozsef)

George III's so-called madness began when he was at the castle. He is now believed to have suffered from porphyria, a blood disorder which has a detrimental effect on the mind and only began to be understood in the middle of the twentieth century. The latter part of the king's life was spent at Windsor where, confined to his apartments, he spent much of his time playing his harp.

After the death of Prince Albert, the grieving Queen Victoria sought seclusion at the castle and became known by her subjects as 'the Widow of Windsor'.

The castle was badly damaged by a fire which started in the queen's private chapel in 1992 but within five years its restoration was completed in time for a ball celebrating the golden wedding of the queen and the Duke of Edinburgh in 1997.

◄ Windsor Castle. (FreeImages.com/Filipe Samora)

NOTTINGHAM CASTLE

Standing on a high cliff above the River Leen, Nottingham Castle is one of the early strongholds built by William I. While it had its share of historical drama from the time it was captured by King John during the civil war of 1215, its most dramatic time came after it became the residence of Queen Isabella and Roger Mortimer. Here, guarded by an army of Mortimer's Welsh archers, the couple controlled England following the assassination of Edward II.

After the late king's 14-year-old son was crowned Edward III in 1327, he found that he was a puppet monarch under the domination of his mother and her paramour. Determined to overthrow the man who had been responsible for his father's death, he was encouraged by a number of supporters who shared his enmity for Mortimer.

Realising it would be impossible to storm the well-guarded castle, they knew they would have to act within its walls. Edward learned that there was a secret passage running into the castle from an inn called The Trip to Jerusalem. The building was hewn into the base of the cliff on which the castle stands and still boasts of being the oldest inn in England.

On the night of 19 October 1330, Sir William Eland, the deputy constable, led a number of the king's adherents up through the passage – still known as Mortimer's Hole – to where Edward was waiting. He led them to the inner ward where they burst into the queen's chamber and seized

Mortimer. Isabella's plea of 'Fair son, spare the gentle Mortimer' was ignored.

In London Mortimer was tried for usurping the king's authority and killing his father. On 29 November he was drawn on a hide from the Tower and hanged at Tyburn, where his body was left on the gallows for two days as a grim warning against treason.

Edward was now free to govern his kingdom and not for many years had an English monarch been held in such high regard.

As for Queen Isabella, no mention was made of her intrigue with Mortimer at the trial. For the remaining twenty-eight years of her life she was a royal prisoner at Castle Rising in Norfolk. There her grandson, the Black Prince, became lord of the castle, but this seems to have made no difference to her captivity.

➤ Nottingham Castle. (FreeImages.com/ Nikolaus Wogen)

ROBIN HOOD

According to legend, Robin Hood's arch enemy the Sheriff of Nottingham used the castle as a court and prison. After Robin had been captured he was held in the castle until, thanks to his Merry Men, he made his escape, perhaps through the passages in the rock on which the castle was built. Whatever the truth of the story, the castle's association with the romantic outlaw is commemorated by a statue of Robin standing beneath its walls.

▲ 'Bold Robin Hood and His Outlaw Band: Their Famous Exploits in Sherwood Forest'. Louis Rhead, New York: Blue Ribbon Books, 1912. (Wikimedia Commons)

Unlike England, Wales and Scotland were not conquered after the Norman Conquest. In England castles were built to keep the Anglo-Saxon population under control, but on the Scottish and Welsh borders they were a defence against incursion by the unconquered.

The Scottish frontier followed the ancient line of Hadrian's Wall while the borderland between England and Wales was a vast tract known as the Welsh Marches.

In order to discourage Welsh raiders, Norman lords were encouraged to build castles along the Marches. While in England the barons were subjects of the king, the Marcher Lords were exempt from taxation and had rights that were normally held by the Crown. They built their own castles and in effect were mini-kings ruling their own mini-kingdoms.

Of the thirty-two English castles that were erected along the Marches, the foremost was Ludlow Castle.

LUDLOW CASTLE

Ludlow Castle, built around 1080 by Roger de Lacy, was strategically sited on high ground overlooking the Corve and Teme rivers. Its purpose, like those of the other fortresses along the Welsh Marches, was to deter Welsh raiders.

The turbulent story of the castle began when de Lacy rebelled against William

▲ Ludlow Castle. (Peter Broster, Wikimedia Commons)

Rufus, the son of William the Conqueror and one of England's most unpopular kings. The result was that he was forced into exile and the castle became Crown property.

The next king, Henry I, granted the castle to Payn FitzJohn. The ownership changed again when FitzJohn was killed fighting Welsh insurgents in 1136 and the castle passed to Sir Joyce de Dinan. He added a circular chapel and had a double moat dug round the castle, the inner moat encircling the keep.

Following the death of Henry I there were two claimants for the Crown – Stephen, the Conqueror's grandson, and Matilda, the daughter of the late king. Although Stephen became king, such was the dissension over the succession that civil war broke out in 1138. That year the town of Ludlow was captured by a supporter of Matilda, Gervase de Paganel. King Stephen besieged the castle and during the assault a grappling iron was thrown down and hooked Prince Henry of Scotland. He was being dragged from his horse when

◄ Ludlow Castle in Shropshire, by an anonymous artist.

guards; a girl named Marion de la Bryere lowered a rope from the battlements so her lover could climb up to keep a tryst with her. When he took her in his arms and led her to a secluded spot, she was so enraptured that she forgot to haul up the rope. Her joy turned to despair when, looking back, she saw another figure appear at the battlements followed by another and another, until there were enough enemies to take over the castle.

Legend tells that realising how she had been betrayed by her false lover she snatched his dagger and stabbed him in the heart. Then she ran to the top of the grimly named Hanging Tower and leapt to her death.

Over the years the ownership of the castle changed several times and during the reign of King John it was once more in the hands of a de Lacy and then inherited

Stephen gallantly saved him. Today the window from where the grapple was cast is still shown to visitors.

A well-known castle legend goes back to the reign of Henry II, the first Plantagenet king. Then there was frequent Anglo-Welsh fighting along the Marches and at times the castle's garrison had to set out to defend the town of Ludlow. On one such night the castle was left with only a handful of by the de Geneville family. In due course it was left to Joan de Geneville, who married Roger Mortimer, first Earl of March. He is remembered as one of the villains of history for having the defeated Edward II put to death in Berkeley Castle and conspiring with his lover, the widowed Queen Isabella – the She-wolf of France – to take control of the country.

They made Nottingham Castle their base with the dead king's youthful son, Edward III, their reluctant puppet. But at the age of 18, helped by his supporters, Edward avenged his father by having Mortimer hanged at Tyburn and his mother confined in Castle Rising in Norfolk for the rest of her life.

During the Wars of the Roses the castle, then belonging to Richard, Duke of York, was captured by the Lancastrians and then recaptured by the Yorkists. After Richard was killed in battle his son, Edward of March, became Edward IV of England in 1461. Now a royal castle, it assumed its most important role when Edward established the Court of the Marches in it for the administering of justice across the whole of Wales.

During the decade following 1472 Edward's two sons, Edward and Richard, lived in Ludlow Castle, Then, following the death of his father in 1483, the 12-year-old Edward very briefly became Edward V. The two brothers – known to history as the 'Princes in the Tower' – were housed in the Tower of London prior to Edward's coronation. Before this could take place they disappeared and their unknown fate is one of England's great historical mysteries.

During the Civil War the castle was held by Royalists but it was not badly damaged, even in 1642, when the Earl of Essex led a great army in an attack on Ludlow. Its eventual deterioration began after William III abolished the Court of the Marches in 1689. It suffered more than it had in any siege after the lead roof of the keep was removed during the reign of George I, leaving it a victim of the elements. Daniel Defoe wrote that it was 'the very perfection of decay'.

After 1811 the ruinous castle came into the care of the Earls of Powis, who still own it. They halted its decline so that today the castle has been described as 'the finest of medieval ruined castles'. It is open to the public and festivals are held there throughout the year.

Over the centuries the borderland between England and Scotland had more blood spilled on its soil than anywhere else in Britain. In AD 122 the building of the Roman wall was commenced by the Emperor Hadrian as a defence against the Picts. Built in five years, it divided the Border country between the Tyne and Solway Firth and was manned by Roman soldiers stationed in garrisons such as Vindolanda, which remains a popular attraction.

After 1066 the Norman kings encouraged their Northern barons to build castles to defend the frontier against Scottish reivers and invaders. One of the earliest and most formidable of these strongholds was Carlisle Castle.

CARLISLE CASTLE

In 1092 Carlisle Castle was built by William Rufus, the unpopular son of William the Conqueror, to bring order to the 'debatable lands' of the Border.

During the castle's eventful history it was once the home of Andrew Harcla, Earl of Carlisle, who was executed because of his alliance with the Scot Robert the Bruce. Mary, Queen of Scots began her years of imprisonment there, and during the Civil War it was held by the Royalist Sir Thomas Glenham, only surrendering to a Scots army when his besieged garrison was reduced to surviving on rats, linseed meal and dogs.

➤ Carlisle Castle.
(FreeImages.com/Colin Brough)

Herstmonceux Castle, situated in a valley between Lewes and Battle, is a splendid example of a 'phoenix' castle. Built in the middle of the fifteenth century, it later fell into ruin. Restoration was completed in 1933 by the owner, Sir Paul Latham, who in 1946 sold it with the result that the Royal Greenwich Observatory was relocated there. Due to 'light pollution' from nearby Eastbourne, the observatory was moved to Cambridge in 1989.

Developers wished to turn the castle into a hotel but the plan was thwarted by the Society for the Protection of Herstmonceux Castle.

In 1983 the castle's owners, Alfred and Isobel Bader, presented it to Queen's University Belfast. It was then

Herstmonceux Castle, painted by Wilfrid Ball (1906). (Wikimedia

Herstmonceux Castle. (Brian Raine, Wikimedia Commons)

➤ Carlisle Castle. (FreeImages.com/Colin Brough)

➤ Carlisle Castle. (FreeImages.com/Karen Winton)

In 1745 it was attacked by a Jacobite army commanded by the Duke of Perth and, after a week, it surrendered. A hundred barrels of gunpowder were found by the jubilant rebels and Bonnie Prince Charlie stayed there for a short period. As the rebellion continued, a Jacobite garrison was left in the castle under the command of John Hamilton of Aberdeen. When the Duke of Cumberland arrived at Carlisle the castle soon surrendered and Hamilton was taken to London, where he was hanged. After Cumberland's victory at Culloden many Scots rebels were imprisoned in the castle's cells.

▲ Castle Rock of Triermain.
(Brian Shackleton, flickr)

TRIERMAIN CASTLE

Stone from a quarry which had supplied Hadrian's Wall was used to build the castle of Triermain, the first Norman fortress in the area of Cumberland known as the Barony of Gilsland. It was owned by the de Vaux family, who, in 1340, were granted a licence to crenellate it by Edward III. Once it had four towers enclosing its bailey and, according to a contemporary chronicler, was 'of great strength and good receipt and a very good place, both for annoying the enemie and defending the country thereabouts'.

In Elizabethan times its lord lost his land and his castle when he was attainted and Triermain was allowed to fall into ruin. Today all that remains is a time-eroded tower close to the Roman wall between

➤ 'The Bridal of Triermain' is a romantic poem by Sir Walter Scott, written in 1813, set in the countryside comprising the original Triermain fiefdom in the Barony of Gilsland in Cumberland.

Gilsland and Brampton. It was a forgotten ruin until Sir Walter Scott, who found inspiration from Border legends, wrote his poetic narrative 'The Bridal of Triermain' which, when it was published in 1813, aroused public interest in the ruin.

It began with the lines:

Where is the maiden of mortal strain,
That may match the Baron of Triermain?
She must be lovely and constant and kind,
Holy and pure and humble of mind.

The legend behind the poem tells how Sir Roland de Vaux, Lord of Triermain, found this paragon in Gyneth, whom he rescued from Merlin's enchantment.

The tower stands on private farmland but can be seen from the road.

THE

Bridal of Triermain,

OR

THE VALE OF ST JOHN.

IN THREE CANTOS.

An elf-quene wol I love ywis,
For in this world no woman is
Worthy to be my make in town:
All other women I forsake,
And to an elf-quene I me take
By dale and eke by doun.

RIME OF SIR THOPAS.

EDINBURGH:

Printed by James Ballantyne and Co.
FOR JOHN BALLANTYNE AND CO. HANOVER-STREET;
AND FOR LONGMAN, HURST, REES, ORME, AND BROWN;
AND GALE, CURTIS, AND FENNER;
LONDON.

1813.

Alnwick Castle is known as 'the Windsor of the North'. 'Hogwarts' could be another sobriquet, as it was the setting for the wizards' school in the Harry Potter films. Like other Border castles it has had its share of mayhem.

Gilbert de Tesson, who had carried Duke William's standard at the Battle of Hastings, became the overlord of the area surrounding Alnwick. Later he joined a rebellion against William II, the unpopular son of William the Conqueror. As a result his lands were confiscated and taken over by another Norman Lord, Yvo de Vescy, who built a motte and bailey castle as a defence against raiders from the north.

The present stone-built castle was completed in 1140 and survived a number of attacks by Scottish raiders. In 1405 it was besieged when Henry Percy, the then owner, rebelled against Henry IV. During the Wars of the Roses it was besieged again but in the next English conflict, the Civil War, the neutrality of its owner saved it from attack by both sides.

After this the castle was allowed to fall into disrepair until, a hundred years after the Civil War ended, the Duke of Newcastle began a programme of restoration. Robert Adam was employed to supervise the decoration. The castle owes much of its gothic appearance to his work, including the lead statues mounted on the battlements which are a striking feature today. It is said that the purpose of such statues of warriors was that from a distance raiders would believe the castle was well guarded.

▲ Alnwick Castle interior. (Jerrye & Roy Klotz, MD, Wikimedia Commons)

◄◄ Alnwick Castle, painted by J.M.W. Turner (1775–1851).

◄ Alnwick Castle. (Bob Whitehead, Wikimedia Commons)

SANDAL CASTLE INSPIRED SHAKESPEARE

Dating back to the twelfth century, Wakefield's ruined Sandal Castle has been the setting for various historical events, many of which have involved royalty. And it also inspired a literary icon. Although William Shakespeare wrote 'historical' plays based on real events, he was no historian – it could be said he was a master of historic fiction. When he was writing *Henry VI* he was inspired to set two of his most dramatic scenes at Sandal Castle. In the first, the sons of Richard of York urge their father to seize the throne when they feared Queen Margaret (more of a king than her husband) approaching with an army. In the other fictitious scene, Richard is put to death by the queen.

In reality, Sandal had its dramas. Of these probably the best known is that in 1483 controversial Richard III made the castle his northern base before the Battle of Bosworth two years later, which itself led the country to the end of the Plantagenet era.

During the Civil, War Sandal was held by the Royalists and endured three sieges by Roundhead troops, which left it in a ruinous state when the fighting ended. Parliament then issued an order that it was to remain in that state. Today the ruin of Sandal Castle is a stark remnant of England's turbulent past and as such is a Scheduled Monument.

➤ Sandal Castle over the fields. (iStock. com/Glenned)

BAMBURGH CASTLE

◄ Entrance to Alnwick Castle. (Writingalltheway, Wikimedia Commons)

The site of Bamburgh Castle, which stands magnificently on the Northumbrian coast, has been fortified since pre-Roman times when it was held by the Votadini tribe. It was next used by the Romans and after they left Britain, it became the capital of Bernica under the Saxon king Ida. His grandson, King Æthelfrith, married a lady named Bebba and the fortress became known as Bebbaburgh, which in time became Bamburgh.

It has seen the whole spectrum of English history – the setting up of Aidan's monastery on nearby Lindisfarne in 634, the ninth-century Viking raids, and rebellion against William II.

Then the castellan was Robert de Mowbray, Earl of Northumberland, who was captured when the castle was besieged by royal troops. King William took the fettered earl within sight of the battlements and sent a message to the earl's lady that unless she had the gates opened she would see her husband's eyes gouged out. The impregnable castle surrendered.

During the unhappy reign of King Stephen the Scots breached a wall of the castle and put a hundred members of the garrison to the sword. It was also besieged and captured by the Yorkists during the Wars of the Roses.

After the war the castle was allowed to deteriorate and in time it was handed over to a charity run by Dr John Sharp, the curate of the village of Bamburgh. Having seen ships wrecked off the treacherous coast he

Bamburgh Castle.
(FreeImages.com/Keith S)

Bamburgh Castle.
(FreeImages.com/Keith S)

Bamburgh Castle.
(FreeImages.com/Keith S)

introduced a lifeboat service and the castle became Britain's first lifeboat station.

Today, Bamburgh retains a storybook atmosphere which owes much to restoration work carried out by the first Lord Armstrong of the Vickers Armstrong company. Its success made it an excellent setting for a number of films.

DUNSTANBURGH CASTLE

In 1313 Thomas Plantagenet, the second Earl of Lancaster, began building Dunstanburgh Castle on the edge of a cliff overlooking the often stormy sea close to the village of Craster. The earl chose the site as he believed it could not be bettered as a place of refuge. He needed a safe retreat as he had spent his life opposing Edward II. Yet when his side was defeated at the Battle of Boroughbridge in 1322 he did not flee to his refuge but stayed in his castle at Pontefract, where he was beheaded.

Later, in 1362, the castle passed into the hands of John of Gaunt who made a number of improvements to its defences, which were put to the test when it held out successfully against a Scots army which besieged it in 1385.

After the death of John of Gaunt the castle was inherited by his son Henry, who became the first Lancastrian king after he usurped the throne. In the Wars of the Roses that followed, Dunstanburgh remained a Lancastrian stronghold until the

Dunstanburgh Castle.
(FreeImages.com/Graham Soult)

Dunstanburgh Castle.
(FreeImages.com/Graham Soult)

Dunstanburgh Castle.
(FreeImages.com/Graham Soult)

Yorkist Earl of Warwick finally captured it with an army said to number 10,000 men.

As a result of various sieges the castle had been badly damaged and nothing was done to restore it. Henry VIII's commissioners reported it to be 'very ruinous' but it has remained a superb ruin, covering 9 acres.

THIRLWALL CASTLE

The story of the picturesque ruin of Thirlwall Castle could be described as a typical example of the Border's feuding days. Standing near the village of Greenhead, it was built in 1369 of stones plundered from the Roman wall. For several centuries it was the home of a stern Border family rightly known as the 'Fierce Thirlwalls'. Later it became the property of the Earl of Carlisle. At one time it stood in Scotland due to a technical shift in the borderline.

One of the castle's most dramatic events occurred when Baron John de Thirlwall returned triumphant from some distant military expedition followed by a baggage train of loot which included a table made of

▼ Thirlwall Castle. (© Robin Kent)

THE TOWER ZOO

In 1235, Henry III was given three leopards by his brother-in-law Frederick II, King of Germany. Henry kept these animals in the Tower of London. This was the beginning of the zoo which, housed in the Lion Tower, remained in the castle for the next six centuries.

Other animals arrived including an Arctic bear from Norway. The zoo was popular with succeeding sovereigns, particularly James I. By the end of his reign his additions to the collection included eleven lions, a pair of leopards and a tiger, which caused a sensation. The King of Spain sent him the first elephant to be seen in England.

In 1831, William IV agreed with the Duke of Wellington that the zoo had become so popular with the public that crowd-control presented a great problem. He therefore had the animals removed from the Tower to become the first inmates of London's Regent's Park zoo.

▶ Tower of London zoo. Once upon a time, the Tower of London had a menagerie. The animals were eventually moved to Regents Park zoo, but, since 2010, visitors can see Kendra Haste's animal sculptures at the Tower, including this polar bear named Duncan. (Wikimedia Commons)

gold, which was guarded by a mysterious dwarf.

As the fame of his hoard spread there were a number of envious Border lords eager to seize a share for themselves. Thirlwall managed to hold out against these raiders but it was the Scots who finally stormed the castle and put the defenders to the sword. However, according to Border legend they did not find the golden table as the dwarf had thrown it down a well shaft. It might still be beneath the foundations of the ruin.

LINDISFARNE CASTLE

Crowning a dramatic hilltop, Lindisfarne Castle shares Holy Island with a ruined abbey. The latter was built long ago in memory of Aidan, the sainted Irish monk. He had made the island off the wild Northumbrian coast his base when he was attempting to convert the pagans of northern England to Christianity. He also established a monastery on the island. As a result the island became known as Holy Island instead of Lindisfarne. The castle goes back to the sixteenth century, when it was built to guard the island's harbour, which could be used as a base for attacking the Scots when it was considered necessary.

At the outbreak of the Civil War, it was held by the Royalists until it fell to the Parliamentarians. The next military drama came in 1715, when it was briefly held by supporters of James Edward Stuart – the Old Pretender – during the revolt of the Jacobites, who demanded the

➤ Once again fit to safeguard the Holy Island: Lindisfarne Castle is much improved after the work of Edwin Luteyns. (FreeImages.com/Keith S)

return of the Stuarts and the restoration of Roman Catholicism. After the uprising was suppressed the castle was to have several roles.

During the Napoleonic Wars it was a fortress, well armed with cannon. In peaceful days it became a coastguard station and later a base for the Royal Artillery Coast Brigade. By the end of the nineteenth century it was in a sorry state of repair. But at the start of the twentieth century, Edward Hudson, the publisher of *Country Life*, bought it and commissioned the well-known architect Edwin Lutyens to work on its improvement. Today it is in the care of the National Trust.

While several castles were also royal palaces where royalty felt secure, others were the scenes of royal murder. The Tower of London had its share of dark deeds including the disappearance of the unfortunate 'Princes in the Tower' and the fate of Henry VI, who was secretly done to death.

Other castles famed for sinister events include Berkeley Castle, where the horrific death of an English king took place; a judicial murder at Fotheringhay Castle; Hever Castle, the scene of one of history's best-known royal tragedies; and the scene of a royal assassination before the Norman Conquest, Corfe Castle.

CORFE CASTLE

When Edgar the Peaceable was crowned in 959 he became known as the Bertwalda, thus being acknowledged as the King of all England by minor kings. In around 964 he had married Ethelfleda the Fair and their son was christened Edward. During his reign he built a stronghold that was later 'Normanised' and known as Corfe Castle.

Situated on a hill close to Corfe village in Dorset, its ruins are some of the most spectacular in England today.

After the death of Queen Ethelfleda, Edgar married Elfrida, the daughter of the Earldorman of Devon. Their son, Æthelred, was later to be known as the Unready.

When King Edgar died in 975, Queen Elfrida endeavoured to have Æthelred crowned but the clergy decided the throne should go to Edward, being the late king's eldest son. He was duly crowned on the traditional King's Stone at Kingston upon Thames. Disappointed and bitter, the queen retired to Corfe Castle, then a royal residence, with Æthelred.

In March 979, young King Edward was hunting in Dorset close to Corfe and he decided to visit his stepbrother, with whom he had been on affectionate terms. Riding alone he was recognised as he neared the castle and the queen's cupbearer was sent to the gateway to welcome him with a traditional horn of wine.

As Edward reached down to accept it he was fatally stabbed. His horse bolted and as his foot was caught in his stirrup the king was dragged down the hill. The queen's assassins then threw his body down a well. After the secret murder Elfrida had the satisfaction of her son Æthelred being enthroned.

According to ancient accounts local folk witnessed a ray of light shining from the well mouth and word spread that it was a holy sign. The well was searched and the king's body was discovered.

The public reaction to the murder can be gauged by the entry in the Anglo-Saxon Chronicle which read: 'No worse deed than this for the English people was committed since first they came to Britain... men murdered him but God honoured him. In life he was an earthly king, now after death a heavenly saint.'

It was believed that healing miracles occurred at Edward's tomb in Shaftsbury Abbey and in 1001 he was officially styled a martyr by the Pope.

◀ Corfe Castle. (FreeImages.com/ martinclay)

Corfe Castle. (FreeImages.com/James Wilsher)

Another dark deed occurred at Corfe Castle during the reign of King John, who ascended the throne in 1199. Having strengthened the castle he used it as a prison in which a number of French captives were starved to death by his order.

▲ Corfe Castle. (FreeImages.com/David Anderson)

FOTHERINGHAY CASTLE

All that remains of Fotheringhay Castle today are some remnants of masonry on the motte on which it was built around 1100. Yet it is a Scheduled Monument and a link with one of those incidents that remain vivid in English history.

While it was the birthplace of Richard III it is Mary, Queen of Scots who is invariably associated with the castle. The daughter of James V of Scotland she was born a week after his death, which meant she was immediately a queen.

When she was 16 she was married to Francis, the ailing French dauphin. In 1559 he inherited the throne, making her the Queen of France. A short while later

the new king died and Mary returned to Scotland. When she had the Catholic Mass celebrated in the chapel of Holyrood Palace, John Knox publicly described her as 'the whore of Babylon'.

The question of the queen's marriage now became of immense importance in Scotland. She chose her Catholic cousin Henry Stewart, Lord Darnley, whose mother was a granddaughter of Henry VII. This meant he was a close heir to the English throne – a point of which Queen Elizabeth I was acutely aware. After the marriage in 1565 Darnley was proclaimed King of Scotland.

Having achieved this position his behaviour became so gross that Mary lost her love for him. She now turned to James Hepburn, 4th Earl of Bothwell, a turbulent Border lord who she had first met at the French court. He became her protector – and lover.

In January 1567 Darnley was killed in his house close to Holyrood Palace. Bothwell was accused of the murder but was acquitted at his trial and in May Queen Mary married him. This royal marriage made him the most powerful man in Scotland, to the outrage of the nobles who took up arms against the couple.

The climax came when Mary's royal forces melted away when faced by the rebel lords' army. Bothwell escaped to Norway and Mary was imprisoned in Loch Leven Castle. Here she was compelled to abdicate in favour of her infant son, who was duly crowned James VI of Scotland – and later James I of England.

The following year Mary escaped from Loch Leven and found herself with an army

◀ This mound is all that remains of Fotheringhay Castle. Mary, Queen of Scots was imprisoned and ultimately executed here. (Iain Simpson, Wikimedia Commons)

AN INSULT LED TO A SIEGE

Leeds Castle became royal when it became the favoured residence of Edward I. Indeed, it is thought that he may have been responsible for creating the lake that surrounds the castle like a huge moat. It was during the reign of his son, the ill-fated Edward II, that an incident occurred that led to the castle being besieged by the king.

In the autumn of 1321, the Leeds castellan Baron Badlesmere left his wife Margaret de Clare in charge of the castle when it was necessary for him to go away. It so happened that King Edward's wife, Queen Isabella the Fair, was journeying through the neighbourhood with her retinue. Weary with travelling, she sent one of her people to Baroness Badlesmere with a request to spend the night at the castle.

For reasons best known to herself, Margaret de Clare arrogantly refused to offer hospitality and barred the castle gate. When members of the royal party attempted to force an entry, the castle archers were ordered to shoot, killing several would-be guests. Enraged that his queen should be so badly treated, King Edward stormed and captured Leeds Castle. Margaret de Clare was imprisoned in the Tower of London.

After Edward met his death, Leeds Castle became the home of Queen Isabella. Later, another English queen resided there – Henry VIII's first wife, Catherine of Aragon.

◄▲ Leeds Castle, surrounded by its huge lake. (FreeImages.com/ David Playford)

of her old supporters, but their campaign on her behalf failed and she chose to look to Queen Elizabeth I for sanctuary. In May 1568 she crossed the Solway and was lodged in Carlisle Castle, before being taken to Bolton Castle.

In London, Queen Elizabeth was troubled by the presence of Mary who, like herself, was a descendant of Henry VII. The fear was that militant Catholics would regard her as a key figure in the restoration of their faith.

As a royal prisoner, Mary was housed at several castles after Bolton, including Tutbury, a Norman castle in Staffordshire. Here she was well treated by her custodian Sir Richard Sadler, who was later castigated for taking her hawking.

However, it was at Sheffield Castle where she spent the greater time of her imprisonment. After the Civil War the castle was slighted and there are hardly any remains left today.

Finally Mary was held prisoner in a manor house associated with Chartley Castle in Staffordshire. It was here that Mary became involved in the fatal Babington Plot. In 1586 Anthony Babington, who had once been one of Mary's pages, joined a conspiracy to kill the Protestant Elizabeth and replace her with Catholic Mary. Letters in which Mary was said to have approved of the plot were produced by Sir Francis Walsingham, Queen Elizabeth's spymaster.

Mary was taken to Fotheringhay Castle, where she was tried on 25 October 1586 and duly sentenced to death.

At first Elizabeth was reluctant to sign the death warrant but after several indecisive months she put her signature to the fatal parchment.

At Fotheringhay Castle on 8 February 1587 Mary, dressed in black, was led into the great hall where a low scaffold had been erected on which was the headsman's block draped with black cloth.

Calmly addressing the assembly of commissioners and knights, Mary said, 'Carry this message for me, that I die a true woman of my religion, and like a true Queen of Scotland and France, but God forgive them that have long devised my end.'

Then she lay still at the block and the executioner decapitated her with two blows of his axe. The most poignant moment came when it was found that her little Skye terrier had hidden himself beneath her kirtle.

HEVER CASTLE

Described as one of the finest inhabited castles in the country, Hever Castle was once involved in a romantic interlude that was to have an enormous effect on English history.

Its licence to crenellate was given to Sir John Cobham in 1384. Later it was owned by Sir Thomas Boleyn, whose daughter Anne had just returned from the French court. When Henry VIII visited Hever in 1522 he met her in the still-famous gardens and was quickly infatuated. Although he was married to Catherine of Aragon, he endeavoured to win Anne's favours.

Anne had no wish to emulate her sister, who had been the king's mistress. If Henry was to have her he must have her as his wife. Meanwhile Henry wooed her with long letters, one of which contained a poem in which he declared:

> Now unto my lady
> Promise to her I make,
> For all other only
> To her I me betake.

In 1527, Henry began his campaign to have his marriage annulled, which led to a convulsion in English history when Henry broke with Rome and divided the country with the Reformation. In return he won Anne's favours and created her Marchioness of Pembroke. In January 1533 the king secretly married Anne – then pregnant with the future Queen Elizabeth I. Soon afterwards Archbishop Cranmer declared the marriage to be legal and crowned Anne as Queen of England.

➤ Hever Castle. (Flickr, © Nigel Lamb)

◄ Tony Grist. (Wikimedia Commons)

THE RAVENS

'If the ravens leave the Tower the castle and kingdom will fall.' This traditional saying goes back to the reign of Charles II, who decreed that the ravens roosting in the Tower should be protected. Today the security of the castle is safeguarded by the customary six ravens with clipped wings who live next to the Wakefield Tower. They are under the care of the Yeoman Ravenmaster, who feeds them daily with raw meat and biscuits.

The Tower of London. The photograph shows cages for the ravens. The ravens' wings are clipped. (Gail Frederick, Wikimedia Commons)

A raven at the Tower of London. (Shadster, Wikimedia Commons)

Yet having won Anne, the king's ardour began to cool, especially as she was not able to produce a male heir, and he consoled himself by entering into a new love affair with the queen's lady-in-waiting, Jane Seymour. In due course Anne was charged with committing adultery with her brother, Lord Rochford. After she was found guilty she became one of the Tudor victims who entered the Tower of London through Traitor's Gate.

On 19 May 1536 she was beheaded on the Tower Green. Tudor execution was usually performed with an axe but the manner of Anne's death was a novelty. Her considerate husband had a special executioner brought from Calais to decapitate her with a sword, a French custom unknown in England.

BERKELEY CASTLE

The castles that were built across England following the Norman Conquest were in effect royal strongholds. Under the feudal system introduced by William I the king was master of the castle lords, just as those lower on the social scale were their vassals. But as time went by the situation changed, as did the Royal Houses, and some castles became a danger to the monarchy when the barons rebelled or when the country was divided by civil strife.

A prime example of this occurred during and after the reign of Edward II. As a lonely 14-year-old, Prince Edward was given an official companion of his own age named Piers Gaveston.

The boys spent most of their time at Langley Manor in Hertfordshire where they were free to indulge in such plebeian pastimes as digging ditches and training dogs. A deep bond developed between them which was destined to destroy them both. When young Edward suggested to his formidable father, Edward I, that his late mother's territory of Ponthieu should be bestowed on Gaveston, the king was furious and cried, 'As the Lord lives if it were not for fear of breaking up the kingdom you should never enjoy your inheritance.' He then banished Gaveston to France but, six months later, Edward gained his inheritance and one of his first acts was to bring back Gaveston, who he created Earl of Cornwall, a title traditionally reserved for royalty.

The resentment of the nobles against Edward's favourite mounted and it was said, 'The King rules England and Gaveston rules the King.'

In 1308 the king married Isabella the Fair, the daughter of Philip of France. The wedding took place in Boulogne and Edward made Gaveston the Regent of England while he was away. At the wedding feast, held when Edward returned to England, he outraged the court by sitting with Gaveston rather than his bride.

Isabella may have heard rumours of her new husband's friendship with his boyhood companion but she was shocked when she saw the affection that her new husband lavished upon him. The king's gifts to his favourite included some of the best pieces

➤ Berkeley Castle.
(FreeImages.com/Paul
Sloane)

of her jewellery. Then, two months after the coronation, the barons, led by Thomas of Lancaster, demanded the banishment of Gaveston. Fearing a conflict with the barony Edward agreed, but began a campaign of 'gifts, promises and blandishments' to get his favourite reinstated.

Within a year Gaveston was back in England and, in the belief that Edward had fully established his royal authority, did not hesitate to insult his critics, giving them nicknames such as 'the Black Dog of Arden', which he bestowed on the powerful Earl of Warwick.

In reply a committee of bishops, earls and barons – known as the Lords Ordainers – set about reforming the government of the kingdom. As they declared Gaveston had 'misled and ill-advised' the king he was exiled for the third time.

Again Edward brought him home with all his property restored. This time the barons took up arms and Edward fled to York, while Gaveston was besieged in his castle at Scarborough. After three weeks of negotiations it was agreed his followers could continue to hold Scarborough Castle while he would be escorted to London to put his case before Parliament, his opponents swearing a holy oath that he would be unharmed.

On the journey the cavalcade halted to rest at the village of Dedington. During the night Gaveston awoke to find armed men in the room led by a man in full armour who said, 'I think you know me. I am the Black Dog of Arden.'

He was then taken to Warwick Castle and on 19 June 1312 he was beheaded on nearby Blacklow Hill.

➤ Warwick Castle. (FreeImages.com/Osamu Kazama)

Although Edward was distraught at the execution of his favourite's death it removed the nobles' cause of discontent, and then there was universal rejoicing when Queen Isabella gave birth to the future Edward III. Then Edward found a new favourite in Hugh Despenser who, with his son Edward, helped him to overcome his enemy Thomas of Lancaster, who was duly executed.

In 1323, Charles IV of France annexed England's French territories, whereupon Queen Isabella was sent to Paris to negotiate with her brother. While at the French court she met and fell in love with Roger Mortimer of Wigmore, who had led a forlorn revolt against the king and the royal favourites. As a result he was sentenced to life imprisonment in the Tower of London, from which he managed to escape by climbing up a chimney. He then found sanctuary in the French court. Here he and Isabella planned a campaign against the Despensers.

Unaware of the situation Edward agreed to allowing his son, the future Edward III, to join her to make the traditional homage to the King of France. After the ceremony she refused to return with her son and the Despensers persuaded the king to outlaw her and Prince Edward. Meanwhile, she was in correspondence with the anti-Despenser faction and in September 1326 she and Roger Mortimer landed with a force of English exiles, disaffected barons and mercenaries.

On learning that his wife's burgeoning army was approaching London, Edward and the Despensers retreated westwards to Bristol Castle. Soon the queen's rebel army was welcomed by the Bristol populace,

SIR WALTER RALEIGH

One of the most celebrated prisoners in the Tower was Sir Walter Raleigh. He was imprisoned in 1603 on a charge of conspiracy by order of James I. While in the Tower he spent his time writing his 'History of the World' and carrying out chemical experiments. He was later executed by order of James I to placate the King of Spain.

> A portrait of Sir Walter Raleigh, which currently hangs at the North Carolina Museum of History. (Alexisrael, Wikimedia Commons)

The execution of Sir Walter Raleigh. (Wikimedia Commons)

NAWORTH CASTLE

Described as 'being steeped in history', Naworth Castle is remarkable in that for seven centuries it has been the home of the Dacre and Howard families. Originally a pele tower, the building of the present castle was begun in 1385 by Ranulph de Dacre, Sheriff of Cumberland. Later there was a romantic note in Naworth's history when Lord Thomas Dacre married Elizabeth of Greystoke, a ward of the king, having 'carried her off' from Brougham Castle.

In 1536, Lord William Dacre was executed for his involvement in the Northern earls' uprising against Henry VIII. In 1603 the castle was restored to another William Dacre, who became the stern Warden of the Marches. Reputed to have hanged lawbreakers on a tree close to the castle, he became known as 'Belted Will'. Sir Walter Scott, who was fascinated by Border tales, explains the nickname thus in a poem:

His Bilboa blade, by marchmen felt
Hung in a broad and studded belt,
Hence, in rude phrase, the Borderers still
Call noble Howard 'Belted Will'.

William's character was perhaps influenced by the fact that at the age of 9 he saw his father, the Duke of Norfolk, beheaded for plotting on behalf of Mary, Queen of Scots.

In 1844 the castle was severely damaged by a fire but the following year was greatly restored as close to its original appearance by the English architect Anthony Salvin. Today the great hall – measuring 70ft by 21ft – is regarded as one of the finest in Britain.

with the result that the Despensers were executed and Edward was imprisoned in Kennilworth Castle.

Here a Parliamentary deputation declared he should abdicate and his son, Edward, take his place. If he refused his son would be denied the crown and a new king found, presumably Roger Mortimer. Not wishing his son to lose the crown, Edward agreed and young Edward was enthroned, with Queen Isabella and Roger Mortimer acting as regents until he became of age.

In April 1327 the ex-monarch was taken from Kennilworth Castle, where he had been treated reasonably well, to be incarcerated in Berkeley Castle in Gloucestershire.

◀ Warwick Castle. (FreeImages.com/ Irum Shahid)

The building of the castle was completed by Roger de Berkeley in 1153 and since then has been the seat of the Berkeley family. When Edward arrived at the castle Thomas Berkeley was forced to leave, something for which he was probably grateful later on as the royal prisoner was about to suffer the most horrible death of any English sovereign in history.

After young Edward III had been crowned royal power remained with his mother and her paramour, who had taken the title of Earl of March. The couple retained two-thirds of England's tax revenue and the nobility began to see that a foolish king had been exchanged for an avaricious

➤ Warwick Castle. (FreeImages.com/Iris Scherer)

➤ Kenilworth Castle. (FreeImages.com/Emma Scott)

tyrant. Isabella and Mortimer realised the deposed king could be a focus for revolt and therefore Edward must be eliminated.

It was then the custom for the body of a deceased king to be exposed to public view before burial to prove he was not a victim of murder. As Mortimer could not risk of any hint linking him with the assassination of the new king's father, it was finally decided Edward should meet his death in what was known as the 'Italian Manner'.

According to Richard Grafton's chronicle: 'Sir Roger sent a letter unto them [Thomas de Gourney and John de Maltravers, Edward's gaolers] signifying how and what wise he [Edward] should be put to death... And being in his sound sleep, these false forsworn persons against their homage and fealty, came privily into his chamber... then took a hot burning spit and put it into his body and viley murdered him but yet in such wise that after his death it could not be perceived how he had come by his death.'

Standing in pleasant Cotswold countryside, Sudeley Castle is noted for having the tomb of a queen in its chapel of St Mary. The castle's complex history goes back to the fifteenth century, when it was built by Baron Ralph Boteler who had gained funds enough for the project while taking part in the Hundred Years War.

In 1469, he lost the castle when it was confiscated by Edward IV, who then passed it on to his brother, the Duke of Gloucester, later Richard III. After his death at the Battle of Bosworth the castle reverted to the Crown. In 1535 it was visited by Henry VIII and Anne Boleyn, two years after they were wed.

When the Henry VIII died at Sudeley, it was inherited by his son, the short-lived Edward VI, who passed it on to his uncle Thomas Seymour. Early in 1547 the Dowager Queen Catherine Parr, who had been Henry's sixth wife, married Thomas Seymour, who had been an early love. Late in the year, when Catherine announced she was pregnant, Thomas Seymour began renovating Sudeley in preparation for the royal birth. When Catherine took up residence there she was accompanied by a large retinue, including Lady Jane Grey, who would be known in history for being 'Queen for a Day'.

In August 1548, Catherine gave birth to a baby girl, Lady Mary Seymour, and then died within a week. Late in the following year of those politically violent times, Seymour was executed when it was discovered that he had been involved in a plot to put Lady Jane Grey on the throne.

Royal occasions continued at the castle when Queen Elizabeth held a three-day feast to celebrate the defeat of the Spanish Armada.

During the Civil War, the castle was slighted by order of Cromwell, but in the nineteenth century restoration work was begun and was completed in the 1930s. Catherine had been interred in the castle's chapel of St Mary but due to the slighting

▶ Sudeley Castle, where rest the remains of Catherine Parr. (Jason Ballard)

of the castle the position of her coffin was forgotten until 1782, when a farmer found it in the chapel ruins. Ten years later it was vandalised and lost again until 1817. At this point the remains of the queen were finally laid to rest in a truly magnificent marble tomb, a royal relic that is the treasure of the castle. Since 1960, Sudeley Castle has been listed as a Grade 1 building.

PENDENNIS CASTLE

Pendennis Castle was built as a result of Henry VIII's break with Rome. After England became officially Protestant it was feared that France and Spain would invade the country in order to restore the Catholic faith. Henry VIII's military advisers decided that the most likely place for an invasion fleet to assemble was close to the River Fal estuary. And so Pendennis was constructed as a defence against that possibility.

As the threat of invasion diminished, it was not until the Civil War that the castle was put to the test when, as a Royalist stronghold, it was subjected to a six-month siege by Parliamentary forces that attacked by sea as well as on land. Finally, starvation forced its surrender, making it one of the last Royalist castles to fall to the Roundheads. As a gesture of respect to the men who had held it for so long, the victors allowed them to march out with their banners flying.

Pendennis Castle: one of the last Royalist strongholds to fall. (FreeImages.com/Pamela Benn)

As castles, so massive and powerful, were a dominating aspect of medieval life, it is understandable that legends should be grafted on to them. An example of this are the castles associated with King Arthur. Though there is no historical evidence that he ever lived, he was probably a Celtic leader who opposed the invading Saxons in the sixth century.

The first known reference to Arthur is in the seventh-century Welsh poem 'Gododdin', while a tantalising reference to the royal hero is in the Cambrian Annals, which described how a Saxon host was defeated at the Battle of Badon in which King Arthur carried 'the cross of our Lord Jesus Christ on his shoulders...'. The date of this ancient battle is believed to be around AD 500.

The traditional version of Arthur and the Knights of the Round Table was inspired by Sir Thomas Malory's *Le Morte Darthur*, which became a bestseller in England and Europe when, in 1485, Caxton published it by means of the newly invented printing press. At the beginning of the book, Tintagel Castle is introduced as the place where Arthur was conceived and, watched over by Merlin, spent his boyhood.

Critics of the story point out that the castle was built by Reginald, Earl of Cornwall in 1145, six centuries after Arthur was said to have fought at Badon.

Today, ruined Tintagel, standing on a rocky headland on the Atlantic coast of Cornwall, makes a perfect setting for the legend. Over the years the castle had a number of owners, the most famous being the Black Prince and Piers Gaveston, the favourite of Edward II, who received it as a gift.

With the passage of time the castle was allowed to fall into decay. Then Alfred Tennyson's poetic Arthurian masterpiece, 'The Idylls of the King', had such an effect on its readers that in 1852 money was raised by public subscription to preserve Tintagel's ruins.

An aspect of Malory's work which ensured its popularity was the introduction of romantic elements, particularly Sir Lancelot's love for Guinevere, Arthur's queen, which held the seeds of disaster for the Round Table.

At Carlisle Castle, enemies of the king, led by the treacherous Sir Mordred, plotted

◄ Tintagel Castle.
(FreeImages.com/tlst)

► Merlin's cave.
(FreeImages.com/tlst)

for Lancelot to be arrested in Guinevere's chamber and accused of treason while Arthur was away with a hunting party.

When a message reached the castle that the king would not be returning at nightfall Lancelot seized the opportunity to visit the queen alone in her room. Malory wrote cautiously, '...whether they were abed or at other disports, me list not hereof make no mention, for love at that time was not as it is nowadays.'

While they were together a dozen armed knights burst in, shouting, 'Traitor knight, now art thou taken.'

Lancelot fought his way clear, leaving Guinevere, who was duly found guilty of treason and – to Arthur's despair – condemned to the stake. Meanwhile Lancelot secretly gathered a band of sympathisers so that when the queen, 'despoiled into her smock,' was led out of the castle for her execution, they rushed to her rescue.

Lancelot seized the queen and galloped off with her to the safety of Joyous Garde, his stronghold on the Northumberland coast – which in reality is Bamburgh Castle.

When Arthur besieged Joyous Garde, the Pope, 'considering the goodness of King Arthur and Sir Lancelot,' threatened to place England under interdict unless the fighting ceased and Guinevere was returned to Arthur as his wife.

Lancelot obeyed the Pope's command, restored the queen to Arthur, and left England.

In the Great Hall of Winchester Castle, which Sir Thomas Malory claimed was once Camelot, there is displayed a circular table top known as King Arthur's Round Table.

◄ Tintagel Castle. (FreeImages.com/Clare Talbot)

Constructed of oak, it has a diameter of 18ft and is thought to date back to the thirteenth century. During the reign of Henry VIII it was decorated with the names and sieges (seating places) of Arthur's knights. A Tudor Rose was painted in the centre to endorse the Tudors' claim that their house went back to the Pendragon kings.

◄ ► Winchester Castle. (Johan Bakker, Wikimedia Commons)

DOVER CASTLE

The military importance of Dover Castle has been regarded next to that of the Tower of London. Its strategic clifftop location was initially recognised by Iron Age folk, and later the Romans erected a lighthouse there. A century after the Conquest, a massive castle was built on the site of an earlier fortification.

Fourteen watchtowers were built on the inner wall while twenty-seven towers were ranged along the outer and it was considered to be one of the strongest castles in England. This was put to the test during the troubled reign of King John. In 1216, it was attacked by French troops led by Prince Louis, the Dauphin of France, who had been petitioned by disaffected barons to take over the English throne.

Although the northern gateway was mined – its foundations dug away – the defenders managed to hold the castle against the besiegers and later add to its fortifications.

However, during the Civil War the castle, held by the Royalists, was captured. A local merchant named Drake led a dozen Roundheads over the north-eastern wall. He managed to persuade the Royalist commander to surrender. A Royalist force was sent to retake the castle but by the time it arrived the Parliamentarians were in full control. As a result the castle was not slighted when the war was ended.

The castle was further fortified during the Napoleonic Wars, when invasion was feared. To this end over 200 guns were installed.

➤ Dover Castle.
(FreeImages.com/Simon Hollingsworth)

The decline of castles began when cannon – known as bombards – were introduced into England in 1327. Until then siege engines constructed of wood were sometimes used in attacks on castles. These consisted of scaling ladders, massive battering rams and stone-hurling catapults known as mangonels. While early cannonballs could not bring down massive walls they could smash open castle gates like long-range battering rams.

As the capability of the bombards increased they began to eclipse the siege engines with their destructive power. During the Wars of the Roses Edward IV besieged Bamburgh Castle. He was so distressed on seeing the effect of his artillery on such a splendid castle that he threatened its Lancastrian defenders that for every shot he had to fire one of them would lose his head when the castle was taken. In 1464, Bamburgh became the first English castle to fall to cannon.

In order to counter the effect of artillery on hitherto impregnable castles, alterations were made in their design. These included curved walls and rounded towers instead of square ones so that cannonballs would ricochet off them.

Gunpowder was also a factor in the decline of castles when it was used for slighting. This was the destruction of a castle by its victors so that it could not become an enemy base in the future. The most ardent castle-slighter was Oliver Cromwell, who doubtless not only saw the military aspect of castles as enemy but also as symbols of a royal regime he had sought to destroy.

Following the Restoration, England's history became less turbulent and the role of castles as fortresses therefore diminished. While castles such as Windsor Castle and the Tower of London continued with their premier roles unchanged, many castles deteriorated when their owners could not meet the cost of their upkeep. Also the fact that the country was governed by Parliament rather than kings and barons made them redundant. Neglected castles became ruins whose stonework was often plundered by builders.

The revival of interest in castles came with the Industrial Revolution and a new breed of successful businessmen who could afford to live like traditional gentry. Their grand houses became the symbols of their worldly success, and what could be better than owning a castle – the equivalent of a private jet aircraft today. In some cases battlements were added to country houses to give them the castle effect.

It was the restoration of castles that led to the popular realisation of their significance in the nation's history.

Today numerous castles – the Treasures of England – are owned or cared for by the Department of the Environment, the National Trust and English Heritage.

ARROW-SLIT	A narrow, vertical aperture through which archers could discharge their arrows. With the advent of crossbows, horizontal openings were added.
BAILEY	An open space within the walls of a castle.
BARBICAN	A fortification built to protect an entrance in a castle's outer wall. It also had the role of a watchtower.
BASTION	A small tower incorporated in a curtain wall.
BATTLEMENTS	Parapets with regular openings on top of castle walls and buildings.
BERM	The level space between a castle and the edge of its moat.

◄ Battlements. (Pearson
Scott Foresman)

CASTELLAN	The lord or governor of a castle.
CASTELLATION	Decorative battlements.
CORBEL	A stone bracket supporting a parapet or turret attached to a castle wall.
CURTAIN	A wall or rampart linking two bastions or surrounding a bailey.
DONJON	The main keep or tower of early Norman castles.
DRAWBRIDGE	A bridge in front of a castle gateway, often across a moat, which could be raised.
DUNGEON	A prison cell in a medieval castle, usually below ground.

◄ Drawbridge. (Pearson Scott Foresman)

EMBRASURE	An opening, usually with angled sides, in a castle wall from which to fire upon attackers.
KEEP	The main tower of a medieval castle.
LICENCE TO CRENELLATE	Royal permission to build a castle or fortification.
MACHICOLATION	An aperture between two corbels supporting a parapet through which missiles such as heavy stones could be dropped on the enemy.
MERLON	A section of a parapet between two embrasures.

◄ An illustration showing an object being dropped from a machicolation. (Pearson Scott Foresman)

MOTTE	A natural high point of an artificial mound surmounted by a castle.
PORTCULLIS	A barrier in the form of a great iron or wooden grille that could be lowered to protect a castle entrance.
POSTERN	A small gate, usually away from the main entrance, to allow castle defenders to emerge undetected to harry a besieging force.
RAMPART	A circling embankment.
SOLAR	The castellan's living quarters.
YETT	A castle gate constructed of iron bars.

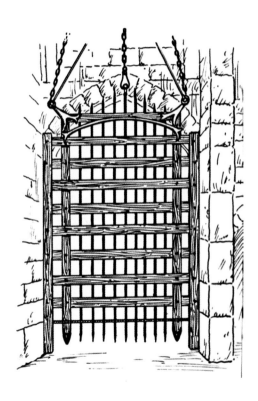

◄ Portcullis drawing.
(Pearson Scott Foresman)

55 BC	Roman invasion of Britain.
AD **122**	Work begins on Hadrian's Wall.
401	Roman Legions begin to leave Britain.
515	Battle of Mount Badon.
875	Viking kingdom of York founded.
959	Edgar the Peaceable becomes King of all England.
978	King Edward ('The Martyr') assassinated at Corfe Castle.
1066	Battle of Hastings. Duke William is crowned at Westminster Abbey.
1135	Stephen is crowned, followed by civil war.
1154	The House of Plantagenet established.
1240	Border line between England and Scotland fixed.

1274	Crowning of Edward I, castle builder and 'The Hammer of the Scots'.
1327	Edward II murdered in Berkeley Castle.
1337	Beginning of the Hundred Years' War.
1455	Start of the Wars of the Roses.
1464	Bamburgh Castle becomes the first castle in England to fall to cannon fire.
1471	Henry VI believed to have been murdered in the Tower of London.
1485	Richard III – the last Plantagenet king – is killed at the Battle of Bosworth. The House of Tudor is established.
1547	Battle of Pinkie – the last battle fought between the national armies of England and Scotland.

1558	Elizabeth I becomes queen.
1587	Mary, Queen of Scots, is executed at Fotheringhay Castle.
1603	James VI of Scotland becomes James I of England. Start of the House of Stuart.
1642	The Civil War begins.
1649	Charles I is executed.
1653	Cromwell becomes Lord Protector of England.
1688	The Glorious Revolution. William of Orange becomes king.
1714	House of Hanover and constitutional monarchy begin with George I.

1715	First Jacobite rebellion.
1745	Second Jacobite rebellion under Bonnie Prince Charlie.
1756	The Seven Years' War begins.
1852	Queen Victoria buys Balmoral estate in Scotland and restores the castle. It is still a royal residence.
1930	Castle Drago, the last castle to be built in England, is completed.
1933	Herstmonceux Castle is restored. Today, it is an international study centre.

AUTHOR'S NOTE

If a visit to a castle is planned it is advisable to check if and when admission is possible. The easiest way to obtain this information is on the internet, as many castles have their own websites. Some castles on private land can be viewed from the road or pathway but it should be remembered that, while it is said that a man's home is his castle, sometimes a castle is a man's home.

THE LAST CASTLE

The last castle to be built in England was Castle Drogo, its foundation stone being laid in 1911. It was the dream-come-true of the highly successful businessman Sir Julius Drewe. The idea came when he was staying with a relative at Drewsteignton in Devon – the name coming from Drogo de Teigne, a forebear of the Drewe family.

Inspired by the thought of building a castle in this ancestral area, Drew purchased a large tract of land and then went to the renowned architect Edwin Lutyens, who agreed to design the castle. The site of the proposed castle was on a high point above the River Teign. Lutyens also designed the castle's formal garden, which remains a great attraction.

The building work began on Drewe's 55th birthday. The building, completely constructed of granite, was completed in 1930. After Drewe died a year later the family continued to reside there. During the Second World War, Drewe's widow, Frances, with her daughter Mary, turned it into home for babies whose houses had been destroyed in the Blitz.

In 1974, the castle and its surrounding land was given to the National Trust. It was the first twentieth-century property that the Trust acquired.